Her Story

Sheryl Weller

Presentation by *BookLeaf Publishing*

Web: www.bookleafpub.com

E-mail: info@bookleafpub.com

ISBN: 9789358312263

First edition 2023

To my daughters, who taught me the meaning of unconditional love. Connected by an ethereal thread, thank you for being the invisible force that drives me ahead.

I love you.

ACKNOWLEDGEMENT

With the encouragement and unwavering support of my cherished childhood friend, Matt Langley, I found my voice. Expression is a way to process and heal trauma and to see beauty in the world. Sharing love, one poem at a time, I am tapping into a deep well. To him, I offer my sincere gratitude for his indefatigable faith in me.

Thank you to Book Leaf Publishing for making it seamless to put pen to paper and create a transformative habit. When we release our burdens, we elevate our level of consciousness, thereby shining a light in the world. I very much appreciate the inspiration of the 21-Day Poetry Challenge.

Finally, thank you to Stephen King, the father of horror, who taught me at an impressionable age that, no matter how dark and twisted the world is, there is always a way out. Triumphant!

Cover photo by *Juli Kosolapova*

Contemporary artwork by *Fía Yang*

Back cover photo by *Erin Gladding*

PREFACE

Stories, conversations, and everyday experiences worthy of retelling inspire my poetry. Written from my unique corner of the globe, I view self-expression as a necessary modality to process trauma, connect with others, and infuse beauty into the world. The poems in this volume are expressive of my journey through coping with trauma and striving to emerge a stronger person.

Innocence Gone

Childhood
Pure innocence
Once bestowed, too soon gone
Catapulted to adulthood
Youth lost

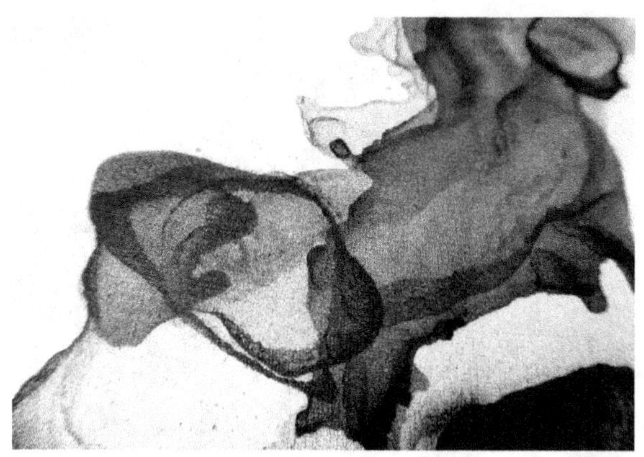

Clipped Wings

Contempt
From a father
Clips the nested bird's wings
Dreaming of soaring while he sleeps
She sings

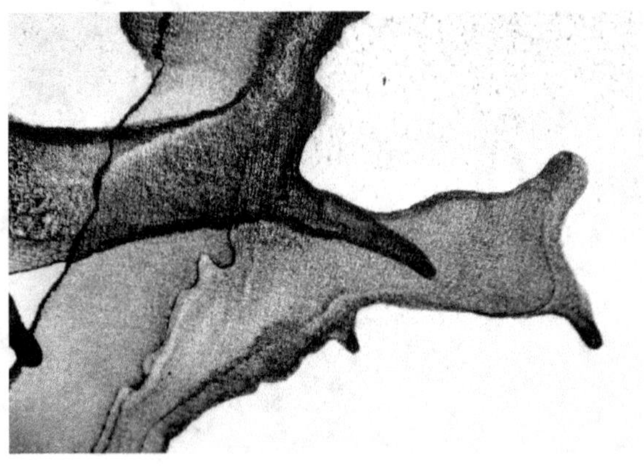

Empty Words

The hum and buzz of the meaningless
Smatter of small talk
Spirals upward from the room
A vortex…an eddy…
A whirlpool of vacuous refuse
Spouted from larynxes of people
Desperate to be seen
Pleading, craving to be noticed
Woefully oblivious
That their empty sentiments
Pile up around them
Like an impenetrable fortress

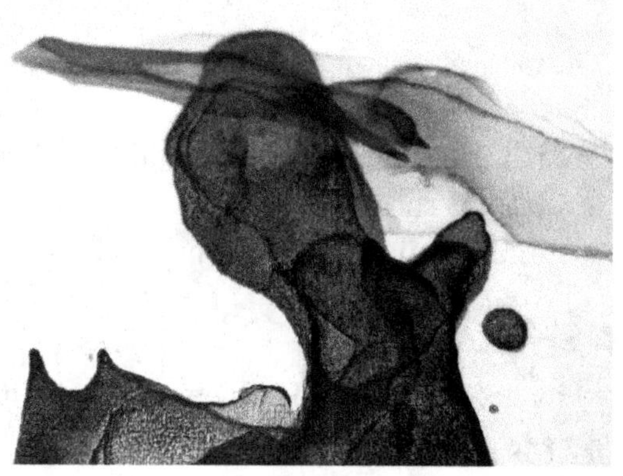

Red Velvet Lipstick

A young girl obediently waits outside, stoic for
her age
She doesn't so much as fidget, though each
youthful thought turns grave
And will soon all be obliterated in a cacophony
of disarray

Midnight displays a voluptuous sky that pin-dot
stars adorn
Ahead in the distance, just half a mile, his Naval
barrack lay dormant
Suspicions soon will be confirmed, though
neither of them knows it

The mother, wearing lenses of rose, is obtuse
about deceit
But is she, though? For deep within, she knows
infidelity is complete
A stiff cocktail of seduction sits suspended in the
sultry heat

Shrouded in a cloak of secrecy, a mistress half
his age
Submissive in her carnal lust and blatantly
risqué

Sex machine of sin at night, personal secretary
by day

Erotic and hungry for pleasure, fantasy takes
them higher
Passionate interludes fulfill their lustful hearts'
desire
When one flame is extinguished, another flame
sets fire

To her eyes were revealed red velvet lip-stained
butts
Night becomes a nightmare, a sucker punch to
the gut
Piercing silence, she screams aloud, "How dare
you!" in disgust

Red-hot rage, as she moves closer, courses
through her veins
Her hands reach out as she visibly shakes,
wondering if it's too late
Can she go back in time through the door from
which she came

Reality slashes fidelity, crimson scar across the
heart
Lacerating with its knife a wife whose sense of
place is jarred

For twenty-three years, it was "Mom" he'd
always called Sweetheart

When she shuts her eyes, she hears remorseless
voices
Taunting her with laughter, ever flirtatious and
boisterous
Reverberating through her mind, she curses her
poor choices

Is this how love triangles end, always in disgrace
Cheeks flush with humiliation splayed across
her face
A wave of sorrow licks her heart, a permanent
scar in place

Sobbing with her head in hand, she stumbles
through the night
Struggling to find equilibrium, seeking a source
of light
Amid dizzying confusion finds her daughter
alone in fright

As they vanished into the ruinous night, a stark
new reality began
The space between them filled with silence, a
galaxy too vast to span
Tragic expressions carved into souls, destroyed
by the same man

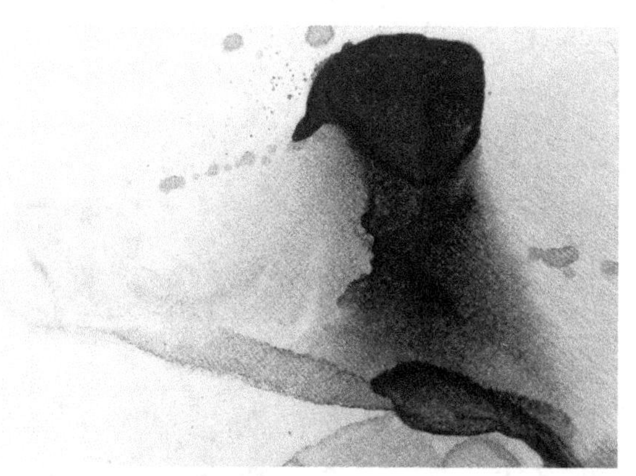

Night Assailant

Haikus
They assail you
In the dead of the night
You must wake up and write, lest you
Forget

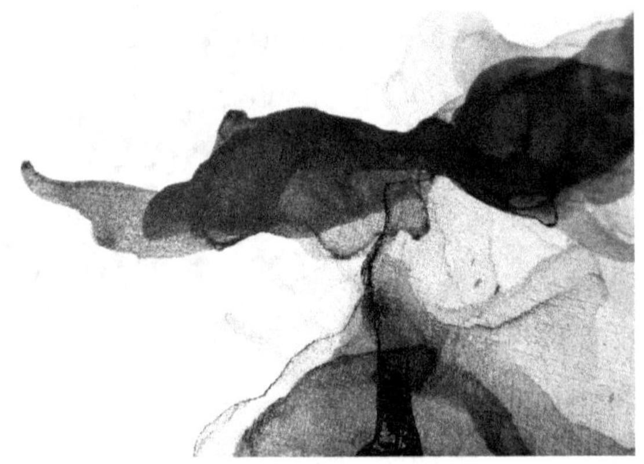

Love Letter

Dear Sleep,
Take me with you
I am yours evermore
Anywhere you go, I'll follow
Love, Me

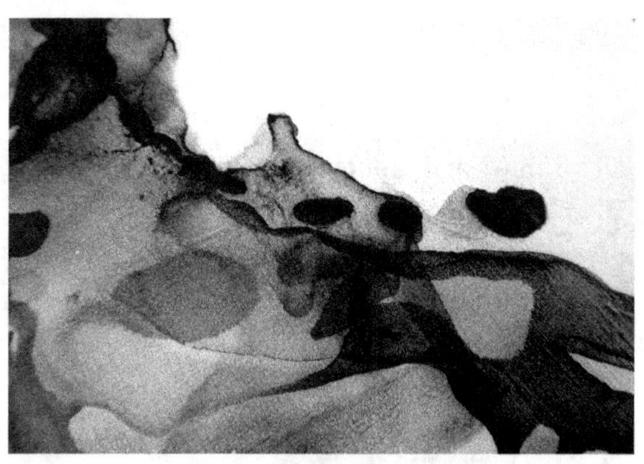

Self-Love Query

HE ASKS:
Self-love?
What does that mean?
Abandon the ego,
Yet still show fondness for one's self?
Do tell…

SHE ANSWERS:
Self-love
Is acceptance
Of all flaws and failures
Wholehearted compassion for self
Freedom

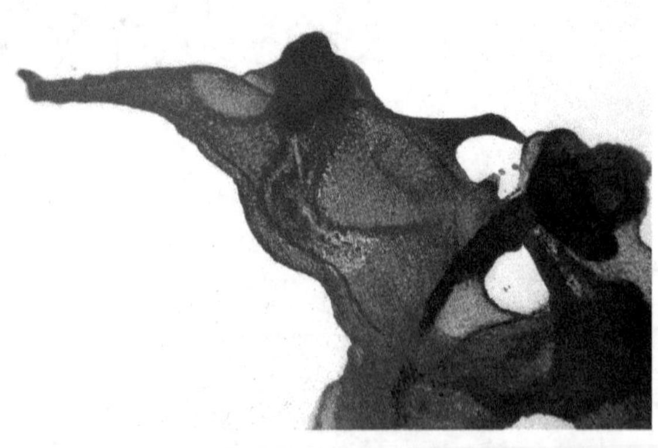

Closed For Repairs

Sign in the doorway makes it clear
That no one is allowed
Absolutely nothing to see here
Secrecy remains shroud

She made it out, moved away
They no longer coexist
But every single waking day
The memories persist

A bond was forged, new lives begun
So many reasons to try
As time wore on, it came undone
A heart began to cry

Weeping, sobbing, silently
In tones, no one could hear
Passive hoping, violently
To somehow disappear

Move on in life and fly away
Refresh, begin anew
To one's full truth, must one obey
To thine own self be true

Fly into a city that whispers
"Welcome…you belong!"
Supported by a trio of sisters
All of whom are strong

Facing fears after fifty years
In a city she's tried to reach
To her surprise, it does appear
Better than she ever dreamed

Sign hangs dormant, dusty now
Soon to be flipped around
She isn't sure exactly how
But new love will be found

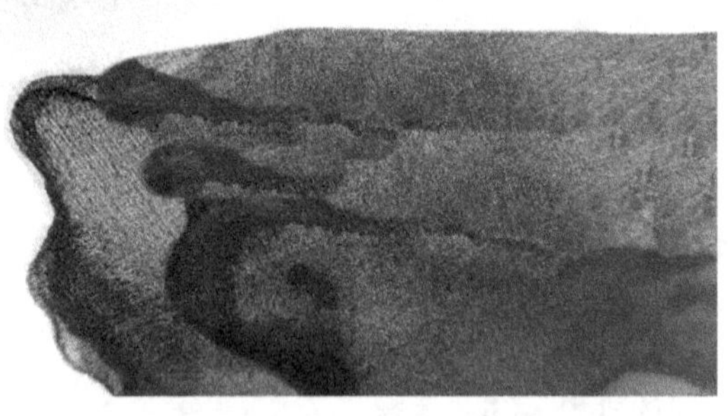

Sandy Beach

Rapt gaze
Sand between toes
Ocean waves, light wind blows
Who's clasped in her tender embrace
Unknown

Something New

Some with trepidation
Some with jubilation
All with expectation

Some wanted, some not
Some bestowed
Others sought

All on the precipice of something new
Something borrowed
Something blue

Some hearts expanded
Other hearts bruised
Locations strewn

West Coast
—> East Coast
New careers—>New schools

What will you aspire to?
Will you come back in June?
I'll wait right here for you

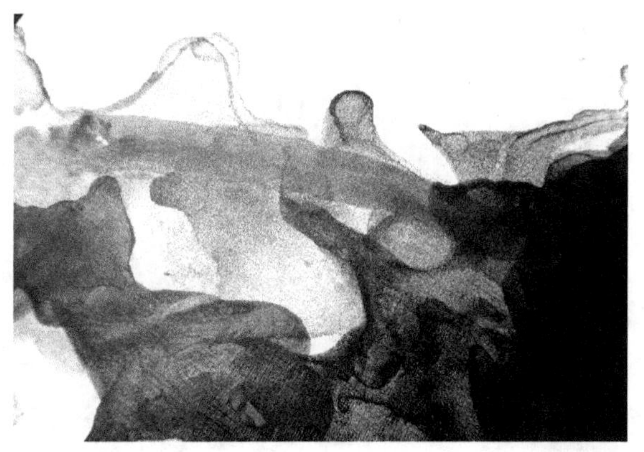

Gilded Cage

My heart
Sits protected
Inside a gilded cage
You can see it, but you can't touch
For now

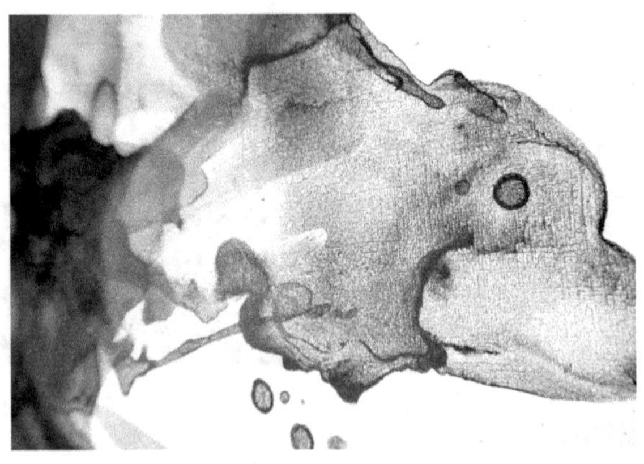

Red Dress

Transactional. Trying to win a woman's heart
with crumbs...dribs, and drabs of love.
Fractional.

Even though I supply you with clues, astonish
me, romance me, leave me feeling wooed. I
want to be pursued.

Absent is any trace of the paradise we slipped
into last night. And as if nothing happened, you
resume your mundane life.

The frailty of humanity has me longing for
connection after our belts and buttons are
fastened. Seduce me once again into submission.

Hastened, you move on too fast, inducing
whiplash. Who were you the night before? I
fantasize about him as you walk out the
door…I'm craving more.

Robotically, you mow the lawn after we "get it
on." I've got my eyes on you. What pleasures
will you pursue? There will always be business
to do.

Switch bodies with that guy! Bring me that
dancing-on-the-ceiling kind of feeling. The
rhythmic tango we ignited had me excited.

Pressed together like two lips, our bodies in
sacred celebration. Tulips. Perfect, deep love.
How could our souls not be permeated?

Rendered colorless now is the shade of love we
made. Fiery, we tore through bed sheets
weighing pleasure with every measure.

Let me put my red dress on. Close the curtains
and dance until dawn. 'Til the memory of
everyday fades and is gone.

Let me put my red dress on…

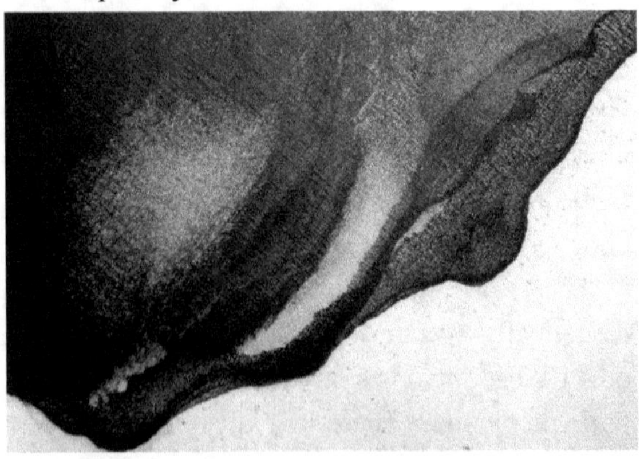

Skyward Trajectory

Buds—the embryonic swellings of the stem
Teeming with boundless potential to develop
Into a flower, a stamen, a lovely expression
The promise of beauty to come will envelop

Physical manifestation begins with one root
Buried securely within the rich soil of Earth
Divinely protected by the sun and the moon
Requiring nourishment in order to give birth

The season is spring and the bud is beginning
A skyward trajectory of life bursting through
An aching—a longing for what it's becoming
What new buds beckon to bloom within you?

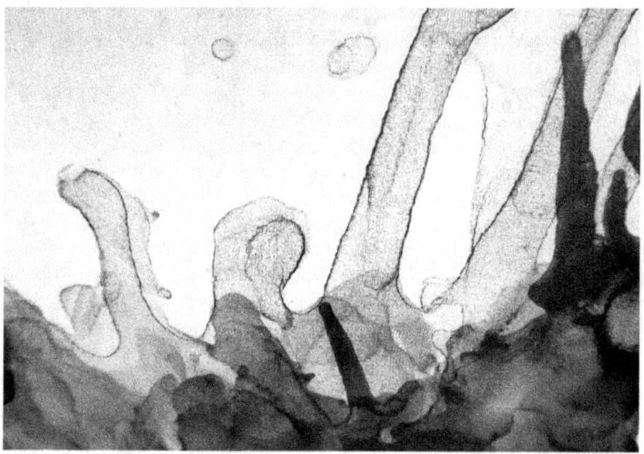

Resplendent Sun

Winter rain is gone
Replaced by resplendent sun
Bask in its warm glow

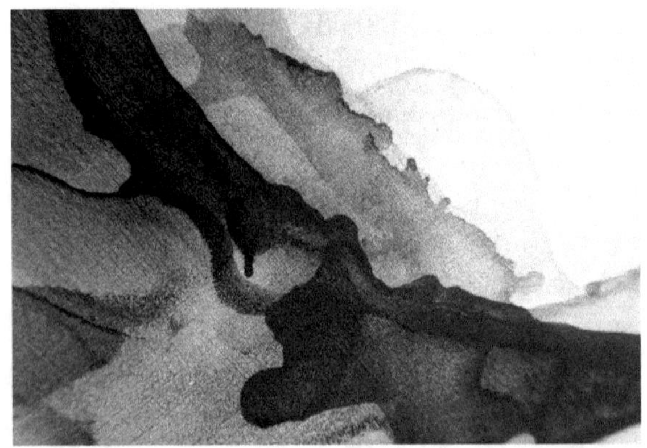

Tiffany & Co.

Encased in glass is a glistening ring
Its cut is brilliant and round
Meticulously hand-crafted and dazzling
The perfect one was found

A circular symbol representing eternity
The promise of solemn delight
No need to get down on bended knee
Or vow love for the rest of our lives

Opening the box in anticipation
Though not from Tiffany & Co.
She beams in joyous celebration
At a pastry of deep-fried dough

Savoring each sweet bite in contentment
Null and void of long-term commitment

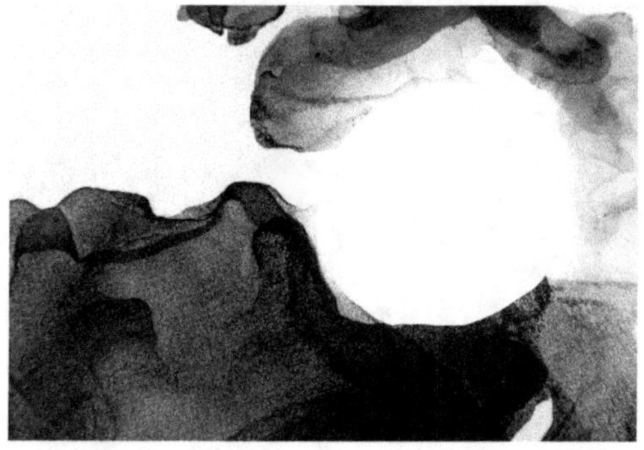

Paper Ephemera

As you sift through paper ephemera
May you strike gold with this tiny piece
Of happy mail made especially for you

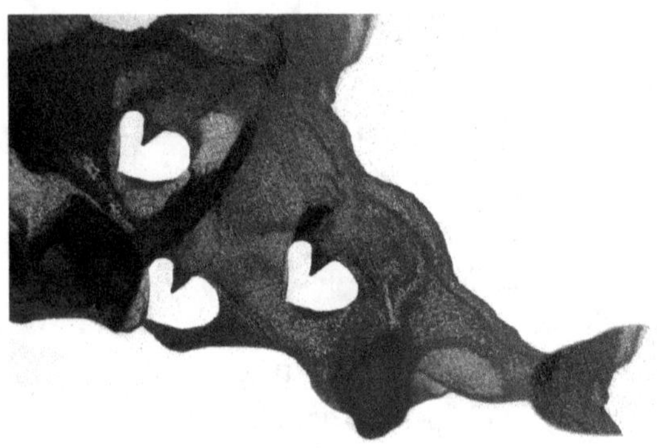

Hands Too Small

It did not kill me, for I survived
His tongue was wet and warm
Unwilling to protect me, idle nearby
My truth would indeed be scorned

A foreign invader, it didn't belong
Something in my mind was broken
Everything about his intrusion dead wrong
Stigma–my parting gift–traumatic token

Parents preoccupied with each other
Though only mere footsteps away
Did not protect me from my brother
Their only daughter became his prey

Drunken fathers and stupid mothers
Must I, the innocent, obey
Prioritize status of boys and brothers
Who seem only to betray

In plain sight, broad daylight
I didn't ask for this shame
No, my skirt wasn't too tight
We share the same last name

Standing near silent, am I a victim?
The world to me no longer makes sense
No one around me will even listen
For my suffering, no recompense

Perverted, offensive, incestual kiss
Subverted childhood innocence
I begged him to stop; I tried to resist
My mouth ripped in blunt abhorrence

Creek rushed past, slow yet fast
The horror of a slow-moving crash
Eyes clenched shut, I froze, aghast
Time stood still; not a second passed

Beyond the force of unwanted entry
Akin to my youth-ripped soul
Why did no one ever protect me
From the enemies inside my home

I turned to look, my spirit cracked
Sense of security on the line
Mom sat rubbing my Dad's back
While no one ever had mine

Like dirt, the only daughter begotten
A deposit of sediment being buried
Pebbles of sand trampled on and forgotten
Hands too small for what they carry

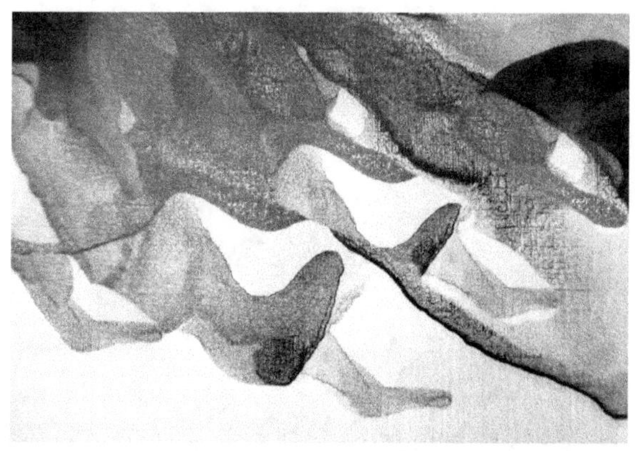

Flickering Light

Her light still flickers
Deep within her soul, despite
Attempts to snuff it

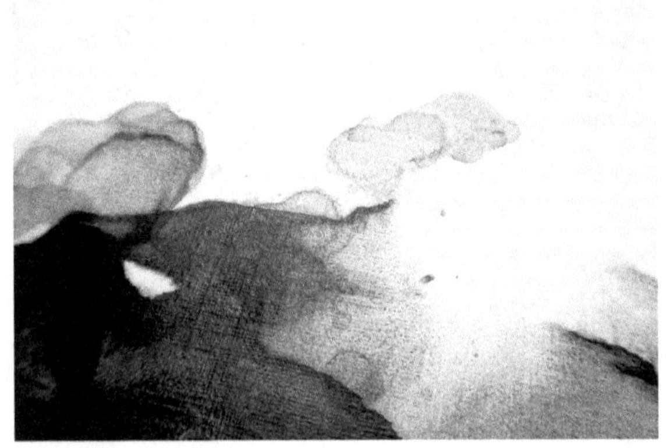

Trees of Life

Palms straight and narrow
Extend into the sky
Trees of life, a tidy row
A Mother's paradise

Fronds ever dancing
From breezes so slight
Once invisible winds
Brought into plain sight

Sun-polished crowns
Where birds gaily perch
Dainty and delicate
High above Earth

Evergreen leaves
Bold cluster of three
In classical antiquity
Power of the Trinity

Poised, luxurious, and tall
A loving heart's expansion
Humble Mother of them all
Megan, Brooke, and Madyn

Each one tethered to me
By an ethereal string
Embracing me each morning
Protecting me when I sleep

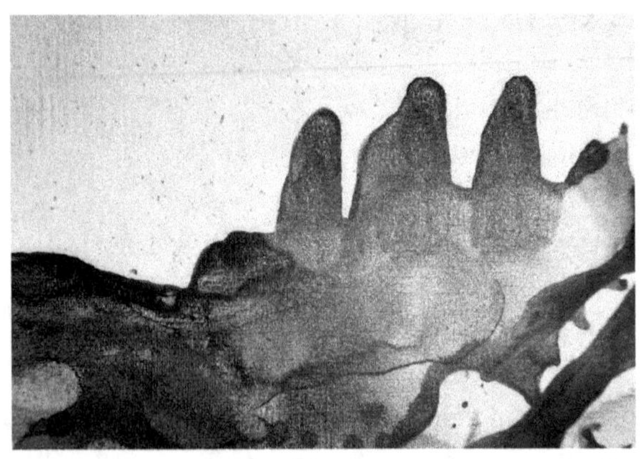

Twenty

Twenty,
Words in this poem
The age I became a mother,
Embarked on single motherhood
And learned about unconditional love

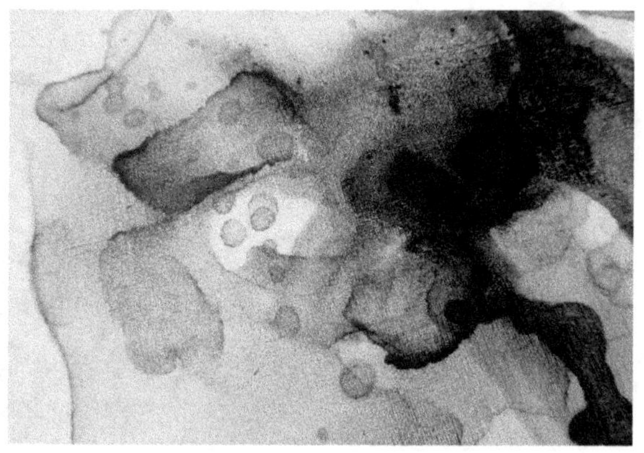

Farewell

My wish for you is
Embrace the flow around you
Allow and receive

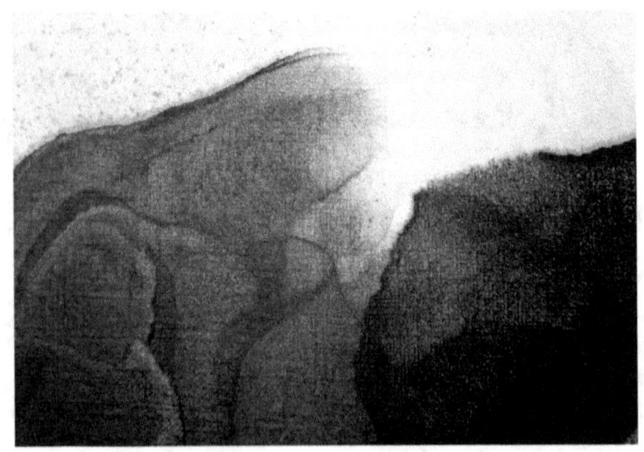